For Genevieve
Artist, poet, friend
on the day of my reception
into the Roman Catholic Church

With gratitude
Anna-Louise +
18 April 1999

Metamorphoses

Jorge de Sena
METAMORPHOSES

Translated from the Portuguese by
Francisco Cota Fagundes & James Houlihan

Copper Beech Press

The publication of this book was supported in part by a grant from the Rhode Island State Council on the Arts.

For information, address the publisher:
        Copper Beech Press
        English Department
        Box 1852
        Brown University
        Providence, Rhode Island 02912

Library of Congress Cataloging-in-Publication Data
Sena, Jorge de.
  [Metamorfoses. English]
  Metamorphoses / Jorge de Sena ; translated from the Portuguese by Francisco Cota Fagundes & James Houlihan. — 1st ed.
    p. cm.
  Translation of: Metamorfoses.
  ISBN 0-914278-55-X (pbk. : alk. paper) : $9.95
  I. Fagundes, Francisco Cota. II. Houlihan, James. III. Title.
PQ9261.S337M414   1991
869.1'42—dc20
                                      90-25636
                                          CIP

First Edition
Printed in the United States of America

Contents

Acknowledgments   7

Introduction   9

Metamorphoses

Ante-Metamorphosis

    Metamorphosis   17

Metamorphoses

    Iberian Gazelle   23
    Demeter   27
    Small Roman Head from Milreu   31
    Artemidorus   35
    The Cordova Mosque   39
    The Nave of Alcobaça   43
    Pietà of Avignon   47
    Cephalus and Procris   53
    Portrait of an Unknown Nobleman   57
    Camoens Addresses His Contemporaries   61
    Elenora of Toledo, Grand Duchess of Tuscany   65
    "The Dead Woman" by Rembrandt   69
    Fragonard's Swing   73
    Turner   77
    Van Gogh's Yellow Chair   81
    Ophelia   85
    Letter to My Children on Goya's Shootings   89
    The Poet's Mask   95
    Dancer from Brunei   99
    Death, Space, and Eternity   103

Post-Metamorphosis

    First Variation   109
    Second Variation   111

Acknowledgments

Although any mistakes or less felicitous translations are solely our responsibility, we wish to thank Mrs. Mécia de Sena for her many suggestions for improving these translations and for her overall advice on the preparation of this English-language edition of *Metamorphoses*. We also wish to express our thanks to Peg Louraine for her careful proofreading of the manuscript.

This publication was made possible in part by the generous contributions provided by Murray M. Schwartz, Dean of the Faculty of Humanities and Fine Arts, University of Massachusetts at Amherst, and by the Fundação Calouste Gulbenkian of Lisbon, Portugal. To both Dean Schwartz and Dr. Jose Blanco, Administrator of the Gulbenkian Foundation, our deepest gratitude.

F.C.F.
J.H.

Introduction

Jorge de Sena (1919-1978) is generally considered one of Portugal's foremost twentieth-century men of letters. Born in Lisbon of a middle-class family, he aspired to a career in the Portuguese Navy. Thwarted in this goal, he pursued studies in civil engineering, completing his degree at the University of Oporto in 1944. Although he worked as an engineer for the Department of Highways for fifteen years, Sena's primary interest was literature. Before he turned twenty, he had already written eight short stories, an unfinished novel, and over five hundred poems. Most of these adolescent works appeared posthumously; others still await publication.

Unhappy with the Salazar regime (1928-1974) in Portugal, Sena emigrated to Brazil in 1959. By then a well-known writer and scholar, he was offered a professorship of literary theory at the University of São Paulo. After the Brazilian coup in 1964, Sena emigrated to the United States, where he lived for the rest of his life. He taught at the University of Wisconsin, Madison, from 1965 to 1970, and at the University of California, Santa Barbara, from 1970 to 1978. At the time of his death, he was chairman of the Department of Spanish and Portuguese and of the Comparative Literature Program at UCSB.

Short-story writer, novelist, playwright, literary critic, essayist, cultural historian, and translator, Sena considered himself, above all, a poet. Including his posthumous works, his published books to date number about one hundred. Of these, over a dozen are works of poetry. Despite wide-ranging generic and thematic diversity, however, Sena's creative oeuvre is informed by a coherent and consistent, albeit complex, world view evident even in his adolescent fiction and poetry. A humanist forever attuned to the realities of this world, he conceived of the poet as a recorder and interpreter of human experience in the broadest sense of the word. He referred to his body of poems written between 1942-1974 as "the 'poetical diary' of a *witness*, as I always wanted to be, of thirty-eight years of Portuguese life." This characterization of the poet as a diarist and of poetry as a poetical diary applies to all of Sena's poetry, although the thematic scope of his poetical corpus is by no means restricted to Portugal or to socio-historical reality. For he is also a poet of artworks. *Art of Music* (1968), a book of poems inspired almost exclusively by works of art music ranging from J. S. Bach to Schoenberg, and *Metamorphoses* (1963) constitute avowedly special sequences in Sena's immense, heterogeneous poetical diary.

In a broad sense, *Metamorphoses* falls within the tradition of iconic poetry, which Jean H. Hagstrum defines in *The Sister Arts* as poetry "of which a work of graphic art is the subject. . . . In such poetry the poet contemplates a real or imaginary work of art that he describes or responds to in some other way. Poetry of this kind may reveal not only the kind of art that a given poet admires. . .but also why he admires it, what posture he assumes before it, and how he interprets the role of language in relation to it." Iconic poetry has a long tradition from classical antiquity to the present: from Homer's description of Achilles's shield in the *Iliad* to John Dryden and Alexander Pope; from Keats's "Ode on a Grecian Urn" to Rilke; from the Spaniard Rafael Alberti to the contemporary English-language poets included in the 1984 anthology *The Poet Dreaming in the Artist's House: Contemporary Poems About the Visual Arts.*

Sena broadens the concept of iconic poetry by including as inspiring models examples of visual arts other than graphic and, perhaps most significant, by utilizing non-artistic sources as wellsprings for iconic poems. *Metamorphoses* consists of twenty-seven poems; only eleven are inspired by works of graphic art, several are based on sculptures and architectural monuments. Two draw inspiration from man-made objects that do not constitute works of art *per se* — a mask of John Keats and a sputnik — and one poem meditates on a photograph of a male dancer published in the *National Geographic*. Seven poems do not invoke any clearly identified work of art. This is the case with "Metamorphosis," already published in the volume *Fidelity* (1958) but, according to Sena, intended as an ante-metamorphosis to be read as the first poem of *Metamorphoses*. The two "post-metamorphic" poems, "First Variation" and "Second Variation," constitute, as their titles suggest and as Sena explains in his extended postface to *Metamorphoses*, a thematic development of the ante-metamorphic poem. Finally, "Four Sonnets to Aphrodite Anadyomene," which are exluded from the present translation, are also an extension of the metamorphic themes developed throughout the book and represent a culmination of its experimental nature. These four sonnets are written not in Portuguese but in a new "language" Sena created from

Ancient Greek, Latin, English, and other words or word roots adapted to Portuguese phonology, morphology, and syntax.

Admittedly, the works of art that became poetical sources for Sena are not necessarily those he admired the most. As he writes in the postface, "it would be a mistake to think that all the artworks and objects to which these as well as other poems of mine refer were the ones that impressed me the most among those I have seen. Many other artworks impressed me much more than some of these as far as I can remember; only they did not become poems for me. . . I asked myself why. And did an answer really matter?" For the reader of *Metamorphoses*, however, it probably does, and elsewhere in the postface Sena suggests some answers, for example by explaining his human reaction to museums: "I know that people only have value as humanity. And the joy I feel, in the British Museum or in the Louvre, in front of the collections where a millenary life palpitates, does not stem from the life's being millenary, strange, distant, barbarian or refined but from my feeling in everything, from the statues to the smallest household objects, a living humanity, living people, persons, especially persons." Sena goes on to say that the inspiring sources constitute the object of poetic meditation —"applied meditations," he emphasizes — as opposed to being "appreciated [only] as mere works of art." It would be safe to conclude, therefore, that for the most part the artworks and objects that occur to Sena as poems are those which, independently of their aesthetic status, are infused with a special human significance for the poet.

As the reader will see, however, these poems are also attempts on the part of the poet to come to terms with many of the aesthetic problems attendant on poeticizing the plastic arts. In *Metamorphoses*, poetic language conveys the poet's complex *experience* of the inspiring source, but it also strives to appropriate, imitate, and, frequently, to supplement the attributes of the art medium under focus. Among the theoretical concepts invoked in *Metamorphoses* are some of those that have guided and shaped the relationship between the visual and poetical arts through the centuries: the Plutarchian concept of *enargeia*, which has been translated as "pictorial vividness"; the statement, attributed to Simonides of Ceos, "Painting is a mute poetry, and poetry a speaking picture"; and, most important of all, the Horatian *ut pictura poesis*, whose interpretation, only vaguely related to Horace's original meaning, has ranged, especially throughout the Renaissance, Baroque, and Neoclassical periods, between concept ("poetry is like painting") and precept ("poetry should be like painting").

Sena's poetry and fiction have been translated into several languages, among them French, Spanish, German, Swedish, and Chinese. Among the English translations of his poetry are *Over This Shore*, translated by Jonathan Griffin; *The Poetry of Jorge de Sena*, edited by Frederick G. Williams; *In Crete with the Minotaur*, translated by George Monteiro; and *Art of Music*, translated by Francisco Cota Fagundes and James Houlihan.

Francisco Cota Fagundes

METAMORPHOSES

In nova fert animus mutatas dicere formas
Corpora; di, coeptis, nam vos mutatis et illa
Adspirate meis primaque ab origine mundi
Ad mea perpetuum deducite tempore carmen.

Ovid, *Metamorphoses*, I, 1-4

Que a glória por que mouro,
De tantos desejada,
C'o mesmo sangue a trago sustentada,
Tendo-lhe oferecida
No templo d'alma em sacrifício a vida.

Manuel Soares de Albergaria, "A uma promessa
de uma glória cuja vida tardava"

Des Menschen Kraft, im Dichter offenbart.

Goethe, *Faust*, 1. 157

Vendrá viniendo con venir eterno

Unamuno, *Romancero del destierro*

Ante-Metamorphosis

Metamorphosis

Next to the thistles, a god lay sleeping
on fine sand that breezes scattered
bit by bit across his body, scarcely
distinguishable along the shore, but breathing.
Sleeping — for how long? How long?
A god or goddess? How long had suns, rains,
and lunar illuminations scorched that smooth skin
where grains of sand lodged in the fuzz?
Black hair streamed down over the arms
crossed over the face. And the eyes?
Open or shut? Green or chestnut in that tiny
place where his breath glowed like favor.
But was it breath? Or just scattered light
lingering on undulating flank,
naked and ancient, robed in nothing
but confident absence in which he slept?
But was it sleep? The legs stretched out,
one foot upon the other foot, heels
raised slightly, a reminiscence of wings;
smooth ass cheeks, curving shoulder blades,
and a suggestion of hair in patched shadows
under the arms. . . God or goddess?
How long had he been sleeping there? How long?
Or was it sleep? Or was he never there?
Next to thistles, almost touched
by the solitude of the sand's immensity,
the immense world, the murmuring waters
— or was he never there? . . . This god or goddess?
Image, memory (merely), aspiration?
From near or far, indistinguishable.

1958

Metamorphoses

Metamorphoses — *Transformation or change of a person into another form.* . . .
If Ovid did not Latinize the word Metamorphosis, *he gave it its meaning to the*
Latins with one of his works. . .

Raphael Bluteau, *Vocabulário Portuguez & Latino*
aulico, anatomico, etc., Lisbon, 1716

Iberian Gazelle

Iberian Bronze Gazelle (7th or 8th cent. B.C.)
British Museum, London

Suspended on three legs (as one is lost),
she remains balanced in bronze
on the discreet museum pedestal.
The ears lifted, as if hearing,
the feet making a reluctant start
while a vacant look strays, distracted,
into liquid rustlings of a forest.
The trees fell long ago. And times
lost without remembrance when
mountainyard villages died
— their traces erased, stone by stone.
And long ago, the people, too
— but which people? — raped, invaded, in blood,
fire, slavery, or simply ravished
by love for men in tall ships
with long oars and billowing sails, the people
vanished, without commotion, trading
their forests for cliffs above heave
of sea by smooth coves or beaches,
their clear fountains for deep rivers
sinuously cutting the green.
This was long ago; the gazelle remains,
with her small fine nose, lithe frame,
and almost human breast. Maybe
she was fit offering for some god? Or was she
the goddess graced with gifts?
Or was she merely gazelle, pure
idea of Iberian gazelle?
On three legs she remains suspended.

Assis, 8 April 1961

Demeter

Statue of the British Museum, London

Monster in vast pleats, no head,
no legs, no arms. A mountain
of hips and trunk. Cliffs
for breasts. Stone, dark with distance,
exact stone pulsing beneath veils
of cloud, of mist. In volcanic fires
she sprouted so in primeval days,
or slowly pushed, pushed up
through gaping crust, so that
she could stretch out along plains
and visit herself in gorges where
she is herself, abrupt, with feet hidden
where seas are compressed black
profundities.
    And yet
a sweet figure lurks under
curves and folds. One could imagine her
white or limpid and graceful
in her hands and fingers, neck and mouth,
eyes, entrails, thighs, shoulders,
life erupting from petrous harmony.

Delicate monster. Colossal weight.
The womb of statues. Life, beneath the sky,
beneath flashes of stars, before waves
coming in gusts to lick the pleats
or pleat every smooth surface, life
breaks out of the mountain shell,
escaping from egg into pure proportion,
winged with the steps the body rises with,
dangling height from her hair.

O earth, monster, stone, soft
robe hidden by veils temporal or eternal!
No legs, no arms, no head,
O trunk and knees, wordless breast,
O statue of covenant, immaculate flesh!

Araraquara, 8 January 1963

Small Roman Head from Milreu

Small Roman Head of the Ossonoba Ruins
Faro Museum

This evanescent, acute head,
so sweet in her decapitated look,
reveals nothing of the portentous Empire:
no tongues meet in empty eyesockets,
no legions march in her mouth,
in the curved nose you will not find
people massacred and betrayed.
She contemplates life sweetly,
knowing how she must, if she can,
refuse thought with a little madness,
for a brief moment relinquishing
the firm tranquility of cool reason.
She is a dream of virtue: the slave
who owned her never, in those sad
moments of having a body, possessed her
beyond this reach. And her husband,
if indeed it was his seed in her, never
felt the weight of this long look
resting upon him. She lived and died
like a goddess among columns, men,
meadows and rivers, shadows and harvests,
theaters and winepresses. Yet
she was no goddess: the empire went on
ravenously swallowing all the gods
it had no face for, so humans,
to humanize the gods, lent
their own which now are lost.
This evanescent head survived:
neither goddess nor woman, only knowledge
that nothing can save us from ourselves.

Araraquara, 12 January 1963

Artemidorus

Portrait of Artemidorus on His Sarcophagus
British Museum, London

Your mummy is in the British Museum
among sad second-floor rows.
Someone found it in a Coptic cemetery
where sands and time had hidden it for centuries,
a calm eternity that you enjoyed, safe
in your coffin not plundered by grave robbers.
How serenely you dried up and how quickly
the "you" that you were vanished
from human memories you had haunted!
No king, no prince, but you were, no doubt,
famous to merchants, friends of long
lingering suppers, and to your wife and children
(though only as infants, seeing you huge and prophetic).
What remains is this mummy: parched
and torn skin, and bones revealed
by unravelled dirty bindings,
like all the other mummies in these rows
under glass, under decades of dust,
London's fine dust, or yours.
What matters now is your coffin or, rather,
the cover where an artist (a specialist)
composed a face for you and your death.
Maybe you smiled or looked pensive,
commissioning this portrait, maybe
church brothers honored your dying
with this noble mask of tragedy, a conventional
tragedy on the stages of another world.
Maybe this portrait was less a mask
than a face that you, or somebody else, chose
for the last act: the finale of being dead
with huge eyes open to fate and chance.

And from those liquid eyes of yours
the look remained to fascinate:
it made the crossing to Crete,
passed safely on to Venice, Tintoretto,
Rome, and finally, in a succession
of apostles, El Greco's Toledo.
But for you and your world
— part Egyptian, part Syrian,
Greek and Roman, Christian and Persian:
Christ Pantocrator, Isis, Pan-Haghia,
angels and prophets, Demeter, Fortuna,
double-faced Janus, Ormazd and Ahriman,
Pythagoras, Plato, the god Ptah, Adonis,
the Minotaur, bacchants tossing thyrsoi —
for you and your world, between the sea
of Odysseus, of Antony, of Paphos, of Cyprus,
and deserts of the Sphinx and the Colossus
that moaned when dawn touched its mouth,
for you and your world, on the banks of the Nile
examined for traces of the muddy murmur
which drowned Antinoos — what could that liquid
and profound gaze mean, that pierces me
glassed over by death, by all these faiths,
by this glass separating us more than centuries?

Listen, Artemidorus. You can hear in the silence
the groaning buses, the muffled rumble
of tourists in more exotic rooms,
but with those eyes, what more can you hear?
Brief reverberations that eternity
(like dawn in the mouth of statues)
wrenches out of us and other earthly things?
The cracks, little by little, opened in flesh,
skin, bones, in everything divine pulsating
into new life through our veins? Everything
that you, serene merchant, maybe never believed?

Lisbon, 28 April 1959

36

The Cordova Mosque

Mosque of Cordova

They had been shafts of small woods
cutting into the blue above hilltops,
or along streambanks where they mirrored
a crystal undulation of nymphs. The fulminations time
and Christians heaped upon them and they fell
strewn in the grass like a sex relaxed in tangled hair
or still protruding enough to penetrate without desire
or effect the wet softness of clouds.
Rose, white,
iridescent, they were called together
for the glory of Allah. From everywhere they
came: in tracks, on shoulders, in carts,
converging on the white city, crossing rivers,
desiccated mountains, obscure plains,
the rain washing away the dust of time
and dust of roads.
Erect arches, raised
one by one, were spanning each other so
curvingly transcendent, so double
in their taut intensity of reuniting
in an immense forest, crowned and erect.
From groves, with branches like wings,
for gods to lounge in, or from spaces
cleared into calm triclinia, they came
and crystallized in the half-shade where off
to one side the *mihrab* is a scream of gold.
Again they support a roof on the potent
sureness of being shafts, but just one roof;
from everywhere they came: blasted ruins,
scattered sanctuaries of gods and men,

to form multiple lines written
in marble and in columns of unspoken glory
of the name that, above human deserts,
is a horizontal roof cool as paving stones,
soothing as a breeze coiling through the shafts,
savage as sparks that could overturn them,
ardent as suns blazing on oranges
ripening in the patio.

                    They came and stayed
a forest made perfect.

                    Allah fled, and left
the white city to flies, dust, and towers where
the voice of the muezzin chanting in the afternoon
turned hard as bells.

                    But who could flee
such a rigid and potent forest: gods transposed
and brought together for Thy glory?

Araraquara, 7-8 January 1963

The Nave of Alcobaça

Central Nave of the Monastery of Alcobaça

Vacuous, vertical, of stone white and cool,
long in light and line, the sequential
arcade of silence, mortal
dawn out of eternity, sheer void
of space fulfilled, needle-pointed
as if diaphanous crystal
of harmonic heavens, a thick, concave
fusion of straight lines, the air sequestered
at the last shudder in the living skin,
stone not-stone that is fastened in pillars
in sheaves of whiteness, geometry
of proveable spirit, proportion
of tripartite essence, ideogram
of mute immensity that shrinks
into a human perspective. Ambulatory
of hushed anticipation.
                    Nave and scepter,
residue of graves, suspended and shifted
storm. Rose and time.
Horizontal ladder. Curving cylinder.
Norm and manifesto. Peace and form
of the abstract and the particular.
                    Hierarchy
of another life on earth. Motion
of stone white and cool, boundary-less
within boundaries. Hope,
vacuous and vertical. Humanity.

Araraquara, 27 November 1962

43

Pietà of Avignon

Pietà of Avignon (15th cent.)
Louvre, Paris

Like a fulvid gold the sorrow of time rests,
in serene anguish that, being immortal, congeals
hands and capes, glances and sky,
and glutinous earth — the sorrow of time rests
upon the five left here with only
a slight sign of death, the moment
its presence passed by.
                              The resurrection
has not happened yet, but the gold suggests
it will, which it is faith to know.
But for those who, being divine, hold
the corpse folded over the lap, like splendor
upon the lifeless limp head,
or like tears that a long cape dries,
for them, human death redeems nothing,
they are part of it, and resurrection
is only the strange transmutation
when someone ceases to be
that body whole long legs,
whose one arm stretched into curled fingertips,
whose emaciated chest and fine waist
broken beneath the hips where the other hand rests,
and whose misery of a dead and virgin sex
(concealed by a white shroud),
will all be less distended
than the irrevocable semiclosure
that life inserts into the eyes and mouth.
In vain, the smooth-shaven donor, attentive
and immaculate, in the corner, kneels.
Mirages rise up from the horizon, and halos
of sanctity are etched upon all — in vain.

Capes sway seductively and sweetly, in vain,
upon firmness whose hems weave on glutinous earth
the uncustomary permanence
of modeled pain. A smooth breeze, in vain,
is tangled in the hair and fingers of the living
and divides around the mother
who holds on her lap the dead son.
Upon all the sorrow of time rests.
They are, here, the generations that day by day,
lived and died unknowingly until the moment
of this death that they had already rehearsed;
and the people who are pain of flesh and friendship
vulnerable to the look so bitter
that it no longer matters
if death is torture or release;
and that man, small and forsaken,
crucified among a hostile crowd,
who dies sighing and gasping blood
that already in his flesh hesitates to flow.
In vain. Though the donor commissions all this,
including his portrait with folded hands,
and though the sorrow of time rests in fulvid gold
to steal from death its perpetual repetition
that resuscitation can never change into life,
faith may yet (its trusting warmth
vibrating in mute colors and contrasts
of a landscape where objects are banished)
betray hope and betray that love
that trickles down the corpse,
livid, as if out of eternity a blood more carnal
than the other which is always blood, coagulated
in the moment when the sign of death
is the last trace of its presence
passing by.

                    At any moment,
in the eyes wet or dried,
when the geometry flickering beneath the cloaks
of those still alive and the heads of those
who are already dead all come alive here
and stare with despair or with the pleasure of forms,
no one but the dead man, folded over the lap,
has any feet in this painting where hands
are as many as the sorrows that love dresses in.
These feet will never walk again,
and, freed, they sway over
the glutinous earth where capes are spread.

Assis, 22 December 1960

Cephalus and Procris

Procris's Death (?), by Piero di Cosimo
National Gallery, London

Of the psychopomp god of thieves and lyres,
lord of the caduceus and the dew goddess,
you, Cephalus, are the son. And a grandson
of Zeus and Cecrops, and a greatgrandson
of Cronus and Rhea, mother of the gods.
Of Athenian Erechtheus, you, Procris,
are one of the daughters — a granddaughter of Gaea,
mother of Cronus by Uranus, the sky, the arrogant
Sky over original Chaos from which Love
emerged, that Eros who was, perhaps,
of the psychopomp and the goddess (who ascended
out of the waters fertilized by the castrated sex
of his father which Cronus cut off)
the son, and so also the half-brother
of Cephalus whom you loved, and who
loved you and, for your jealousy, killed you.

For mere jealousy? No. For if Cephalus
returns disguised by the Dawn who had abducted him,
and Procris cheats on him with himself;
and if, when he reveals who he is, she flees
to Artemis to win the unerring spear
and the dog faster than the wind that she will give
to him when they meet again, later,
and she is the transformed stranger;
if she hides to spy on one breeze
who enfolds him, grazing his skin with kisses;
if a slight rustling betrays her and makes
the spear in the hand of Cephalus pierce her,
while the dog contemplates these demigods

who, like the gods, destroy one another;
if the immense beach is by animals trod
who live easy and foreign beneath the sky;
if the husband is almost a satyr mourning
the dead nymph who couldn't be Procris;
if the sharpness of traces is prolonged
into luminescent shade where the ill-omened
generation of gods persists; if
of deceptions, of mutations, of incest, of crimes
comes the freedom of being born human,
"not of the sky, not of earth, not mortal,
or immortal, but free and proud like an artist
who sculpts his own being and patterns it
in the chosen form";

                           then the song and the death,
and the plunder and the gift, and the sweet dew
on morning leaves (like foam washed up
on the beach from the semen of Cronus)
and chisel and stone, aspect and pattern,
that unknown pattern, between things and their becoming
which perishes, free, when Procris dies,
and remains, proud, when Cephalus is the killer.

Assis, 9 March 1961

Portrait of an Unknown Nobleman

Portrait of a Young Nobleman
Portuguese School, 16th cent.
Museu Nacional de Arte Antiga, Lisbon

He fixes us, as the painter conceived,
as he never fixed anyone before.
Family and friends found "a resemblance" in the portrait,
but he never recognized himself.
The master, years later, by chance
saw the splendid canvas without turning
to see the model, and found what he'd made
bad art. He didn't see
that profound stare, so variable, so different
from the swirled tones with which he covers the world.

But this is merely speculation.

Who was he? We don't even know his name,
we know absolutely nothing. A clear
forehead, a mouth closing in vague disdain,
eyes with irony counterfeiting youth,
blackness, rosiness, terra cotta, the easy
brushstrokes all seem to speak. Only seem to.
Of him, as of the Master, we know
absolutely nothing. And the date?
Also quite uncertain.

Magnificent portrait. Yes, no doubt,
of an important person. And do we still
depend on this youth? And who was he?
Did he know? Or could the painter have known
in that moment when eyes alone contain the world?

Lisbon, 28 August 1958

Camoens Addresses His Contemporaries

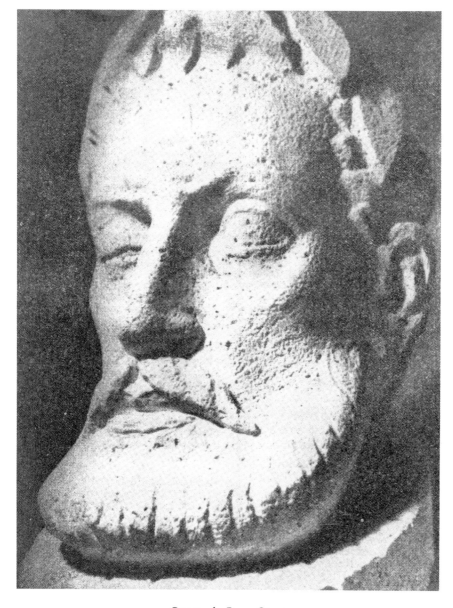

Camoens, by Bruno Giorgi
Ministério da Educação do Brasil, Rio de Janeiro

You can steal everything from me:
my phrases, images, ideas,
my metaphors, motifs, my themes,
my symbols, and even my superiority
in suffering pains of a new language
in understanding another, in the courage
to fight, judge, penetrate the inner sanctum
of love where all you eunuchs cannot go.
And later, you can refuse to cite me,
suppress or ignore me, envying
other thieves luckier than yourselves.
It doesn't matter. Your sentence
will be horrible: for when your grandchildren
have already forgotten who you are,
they will have to know me even better
than you feign not to know,
and everything, everything you studiously pilfer,
will be reclaimed by my name. Even
the miserable particle of invention
that you squeezed out on your own, without theft,
even that will be mine, considered mine, counted mine.
You will have nothing upon nothing:
even your skeletons will be looted for bones
to pass for mine. So that other thieves,
like you, on their knees, can put flowers on my tomb.

Assis, 11 June 1961

Elenora of Toledo, Grand Duchess of Tuscany

to Murilo Mendes

Eleonora di Toledo, by Bronzino
Wallace Collection

Pompous and dignified, officially joyless,
she is ideal geometry for banking princes
and their European nephews, cousins, uncles,
kings, lords of lands and oceans,
who have struck a perfect, severe balance
between sex, devotion, and mortgages.
The world is a huge harbor of strict intolerance
where slaves, pepper, and charity
are sheltered in the shade of columns
without a trace of barbarous Gothic.
In the firm mouth as in the obdurate glance,
in hair pulled back into fierce knots,
in pearls upon pearls on breasts
scarcely raising the embroidery,
there is a cold virtue, a science
of not sinning in confessional or bed,
and a reserve of distant enchantment
where Reason of State was a proud stroll
by trees of a sandy garden on walks and lawns
arranged according to the golden mean.
No doubt the stars, by a science
of already rounded earth, laid out
the guiding proportions of the painting.
Palaces, feasts, complicated odes,
processions, and scaffolds, and the
Tuscan-sky clarity hovering
over dust and ruins of imperial Toledo,
all this is compressed into a penetrating tone
of ambiguous ocher where colors oppose one another
like the very practical theses painstakingly

wrought at Trent for the eternal repose
of Christian princes who devour one another
beneath the paternal care of ethereal Rome
guarded by cardinals, friars, and the Swiss.
This grand duchess — it hardly matters, before the canvas,
if she really was a grand duchess, or whose daughter
or mother she was — had herself painted.
But the painting was something else, a shield,
a family crest, an inlaid buckler
for easing into death when anguish rises
like a vomit of blood from the simple fact
of having a soul (or not), of worlds being multiple,
of the Sun turning around the whole earth (or not),
illuminating multitudes, races, everything,
princes and subjects, in that harmony of the world,
whose silent scream can be heard at dawn
creaking discretely, in the castle gates.

Lisbon, 6 June 1959

"The Dead Woman" by Rembrandt

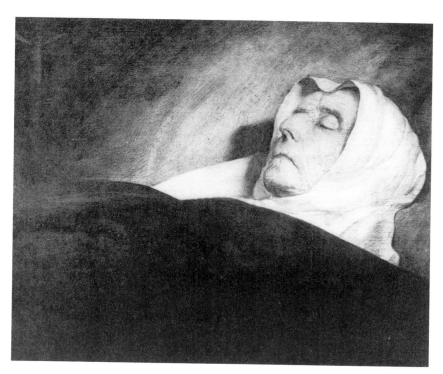

The Dead Woman, by Rembrandt
Musée National d'Art Ancien, Brussels

Dead. Simply dead. Nothing more than dead.
She is not asleep, and don't say
she dreams or rests, or got from life
what she never lived. Dead, she appears,
and nothing more appears. Everything is composed,
disposed, to find a harmony
so death is hers, simply.

She is old. Old, or consumed by the serene pain
of waiting for life to weaken, blow by blow,
the links between memory and flesh,
between piety, pleasure, and the simple
listening to others, how they laugh or cry
or whisper or hear themselves in silence
as she heard herself in a calm distraction
of breathing the time her veins pulse with.

Every type of life is utterly put out.
First, the life that was hers and was,
as it were, shared with all she loved,
with acquaintances, or those vague faces
barely remembered as shadows of pensive days
when the eye suddenly stops
upon what passes by, or doesn't. And then
the life that dwelt in her but was not hers:
the unnameable living and being alive,
the inherited life that centuries of bodies
have possessed from the primordial and swampy night
down to the room where she cried, being born.

Forms of life there are, but none subsists
in the circle of light around her face
so marbled in the white shroud, so removed
from the dark cover. She cannot
have been dead long, but already in her mouth,
arched like the eyebrows or tapering hook
of the nose, already in her fine-lipped mouth,
nothing palpitates, not even death.

The light does not reach a crucifix
that hangs on the wall at the foot of the bed,
but on her face the light stops sharp and mild,
brightening the web of a thousand wrinkles
woven by the spider that spins
between us and others, between us and things,
between us and ourselves, even when life was not
the shivering of skin beneath a gliding kiss,
nor a glancing wind, an unrecognized
anxiety, a sudden fear,
a hesitancy before sad confidences.

She is dead. Simply dead. Yet
in the solitude that even colors cannot resist
the world does not die, Death is not present,
nothing is present by this woman
who has stopped being the solitude of life
so she could stay here, before rotting,
in this moment when agony fails
and solitude — we finally see! — is visible
in the yellowish face, in the white shroud,
in the dark cover, in the circle of light,
in the resting place of the head,
and in the heavy thick lids
closed upon her eyes forever.

Lisbon, 12 May 1959

Fragonard's Swing

The Swing, by Fragonard
Wallace Collection

How she swings into air in the space
between the flutter of her indiscreet skirts
and the quivering grove! What flashes
of half-seen legs, what more unseen
by the man relaxing into his indiscreet
pleasure of revealing himself hidden!
What glances! Her air-borne shoe
in light suffused like a burning cloud
of visceral throbbing in the leaves!
How this garden is seeded with voluptuousness
entwined around the trees and the poses
and the pointing fingers and shadows!
How many skirts remain and constrain
the sex and breasts, swelling prisoners
divined by his sharp cattiness!
How statues and walls swing in the vertigo
of ropes so horny they might
grace a lucky husband!
O how she swings and flutters! How fashionable
the lover and his pose — and his obscene
delight in only looking!
How his eyes undress her, and how she resists
with a cutting and wry glance,
knowing how much lace there is to tear!
How nothing else in the world matters!

Assis, 8 April 1961

Turner

Slave Ship, by Turner
Museum of Fine Arts, Boston

In silent fog where noises crisscross
like beams of light through a prism broken,
there is a gold margin of mute reflections
in the suspensive vibration of dusky water,
which vague shapes enkindle with flapping sails
and flags spread by a wind just foretold
for the shred marine sky spreading over stone cities
dissolved into stairways that shelter clouds
and the sifted Sun
and bonfires and light of the Moon.

Undulant vague shapes (sinuous, cool,
yielding to rips in the mist that,
when ripped, composed them)
are windows giving out onto domes
and fields and groves of autumn quiet
where green is a gold parched
by the smoky brilliance of twilight
of evenings or dawns they are confused with
in the same humanity without contours,
just force and shadow like ships
drifting without mast without sails
billowing full and transparent over the deep
in orange and gray resonance
of the steaming rivermouth where tides
thicken with remembered deep-sea tempests
with their gray-foamed waves,
while gaping stained furnaces, bridges,
and a Venetian cushion are washed downstream,
and the galleys of Odysseus
are the horizon and a shrewd elegance.

What a silence of light seen head-on,
gazed at against colors on this side of forms,
on this side of vibrations changing
into surface and taut volumes!
How like a stain over the canvas
the piercing and greedy blindness spreads,
that gnaws at the sea-surge of worlds!
And beyond this serene noise
that thickens what is tenuous into swirls,
nothing else exists. Not even painting.

Lisbon, 19-20 June 1959

Van Gogh's Yellow Chair

The Yellow Chair, by Van Gogh
National Gallery, London

On the tilework, a rustic chair
rustically caned, yellow
above worn and refired tiles.
On the seat of the chair, a pipe and a touch of tobacco
(or something) wrapped in paper or a kerchief.
On a tinderbox, close behind, the signature.
What more? The faded door, once azure.
"Vincent," so he signed, and out of dense matter,
where brushstrokes are sweetly enjambed,
the elegant curve takes shape, and each of the chair's
cross-supports swells like the rich clay
in the filthy, infested, uneven tiles.

But after goddesses, dead rabbits,
battles, princes, forests,
flowers in jars, meandering rivers,
and the calm chiaroscuro of Dutch interiors,
there was still a need for this humility: the cane seat
where a modest vice — tobacco — was forgotten
or was carefully arranged as a sign
that those who want everything
are soon content with almost nothing.

Yet it is not a yellow chair, whatever else
that piece of meager furniture was in an empty room
where madness was a piety in the extreme,
because of the people who pass outside,
laugh outside but don't want ears to hear,
don't want, even on a gilded platter, the severed lobe
still quivering in a spot of blood,

don't want the *quantum satis*
of faithfulness, dedication, love, restraint,
anxiety, vigils, and, above all,
don't want the penetrating gaze
of intoxicating and pure solitude.

It never was, is, or will be a chair:
rather the portrait, lucid and focused,
of there having been someone who essentially was,
who knew the chair by gazing and by sitting
in the small room of nothing but color, not even light,
and a tinderbox in the corner signed "Vincent."

A given name, a pipe, a closed door,
a floor that slips out from under your feet
when, in the close space, you fix your gaze on the chair
— the chair that was humble
with the same humility he knew was devouring
from within his inner self,
which he possessed for no other reason
than a given name, a thing children
desperately believe in, growing up,
as they do, on the outskirts of madness.
There is someone who signs
on a box in the corner his crow name.*
And there are corners in painting?
Perpetual names? And what chair, or non-chair,
is really humble? Every chair, or just this one?
At the end, will only chairs remain,
and the modest vice posed on the seat
for as long as colors can still thicken?

Lisbon, 21 May 1959

---

*"St. Vincent" is a name used in Portugal to refer to the crow. Legend has it that the saint,
who is the patron of Lisbon, traveled to the city on a boat accompanied by crows.
(Translators' note.)

Ophelia

Ophelia, by Fernando de Azevedo
Jorge de Sena Collection

Red flame with yellow streaks
running over lagoon waters
on the edge of a whitened beach where
walls are mirrored in still waters
and, also, in the quivering reflections
of the blue and, when kindled, green butterfly
— O mist of castles, suspensive sky,
O azure dark sky, O Elsinore,
"have you a daughter? Let her not walk in the sun:
conception is a blessing but not
as your daughter may conceive. Friend, look to 't."

The scene, my lords: an indigo sky,
with tempest clouds where whiteness
strikes the observer and the beach
that walls keep to an easy windy rippling
along clifftops that slip away
like reflections of a wing or royal cape
airily hanging from invisible shoulders
— the scene, the stage: "indifferent children;
I loved you once; briefly, my lord,
be chaste as ice, pure as snow;
what a fair thought to lie between
a maid's legs!"

A maid's legs, O thin flames
that a breath puts out, that open, when touched,
for the rigid sex kindling the sweet
pink lips crowned by curls darker
that the long, long loosened hair!
"Before you had me, you promised
to marry me. Come, my coach!"

Balconies and fog and turbid walls
and a colored and raw anxiety
softly insinuated by strokes
of a penetrated virgin possession. Ophelia!
"For some must watch, while others sleep.
Good night, sweet prince, and flights of angels
sing thee to thy rest."

Bloodily the butterfly dissolves
and is lost along the mild waters.

Lisbon, 20 June 1959

Letter to My Children on Goya's Shootings

Third of May, by Goya
Prado, Madrid

I don't know, my children, what world you'll have.
It's possible, for everything is possible, that you'll have
the world I want for you. A simple world
with only one difficulty being that nothing
is not simple and natural.
A world where everything is permitted,
after your taste, yearning, and pleasure,
and respect for others and theirs for you.
And it's possible that it's not this, not even this
that interests you in living. Everything is possible,
even when we struggle, as we must,
for what seems to be freedom and justice
and, even more, a faithful devotion
to the honor of being alive.
One day, you'll know that more than humanity
they are numberless who thought thus,
who loved their fellows for what in them was unique,
uncustomary, free, different,
and who were sacrificed, tortured, beaten,
hypocritically delivered to secular justice for liquidation
"with utmost piety, without bloodshed."
And for being faithful to a god, a thought,
a country, a hope, or only
an insatiable hunger devouring them from within,
they were disemboweled, flayed, burned, gassed,
their bodies heaped up as anonymously as they'd lived,
or their ashes scattered so that no memory of them would remain.
And sometimes, for being of a race
or, at other times, a class, they paid in full
for crimes they never commited or were never aware

of having committed. And yet it happened,
and still happens, that they were not killed.
There have always been infinite modes of prevailing,
of annihilating gently and delicately through trackless
paths as those of God are said to be trackless.
These shootings, this heroism, this horror
were one thing among a thousand in Spain
more than a century ago, and the violence and injustice
offended the heart of a painter named Goya,
who had a huge heart of rage
and love. But, my children, this is nothing.
Only an episode, a brief episode
in the chain where you form one link (or not)
of iron, sweat, blood, and a drop of semen
on the path of the world I dream for you.
Believe me that no world, nothing, nobody
has more value than a life or the joy of having it —
and this joy is what matters.
Believe that the dignity you will hear so much about
is finally nothing but this joy arising
from being alive and knowing that no one ever
suffers or dies or is less alive so that
any one of you can resist, a little longer, the death
that belongs to all and comes for all.
My fervent hope is that you will know all this calmly,
blaming no one, with no fear or greed
or, worse, indifference or detachment.
So much blood, pain, and anguish someday
(even if the tedium of a happy world troubles you)
will not have been in vain. Yet I confess that often,
recalling so many years of cruelty and subjugation,
I hesitate for a moment, crushed in bitterness,
and I am inconsolable. Are they really
not in vain? And even if they aren't,
who will bring back those millions, restore
not simply their lives but all that was stolen from them?

No Final Judgment, my children, can give back
that moment they never lived, that object
never enjoyed, that motion of love
always reserved for "tomorrow."
And so let us hold with care
the very world we may create, hold it as something
not ours but granted to us to guard with respect,
in memory of the blood within our flesh,
of the flesh that was once another's, and of the love
with which others never loved because it was stolen.

Lisbon, 25 June 1959

The Poet's Mask

Keats's Bronze Mask
National Portrait Gallery, London

You closed your eyes as if you were dying
and calmly sealed mouth and lips
and finally the yearning silent lids
concealing the look that seemed about to speak.
They came and cast your mask in bronze,
modeled it from your face, live or dead.
It's not a work of art, it's you.
No portrait, no artist groping for essence,
no *materiel* the master feels
guiding and seducing his hands,
as matter always does. It's you.
Carnality and blood, the sense of being,
thought knifing into things,
anguish, love, death that glides by so close,
and the thing of beauty, an eternal joy
— all this would have poured throbbing into the bronze,
if the bronze had really been the skin
of your face, that moment the mold was poured.
And yet all this did throb beneath your face,
and oppress, and slowly murder you.
And the killer's hands were verse
distant and coy as Fanny Brawne.

You knew all this, and your face shows it
in this sharp profile of bronze
that gleams brilliantly as pearls polished
by the vital sweat of your anguish.
For to you, poetry was a strange dormancy
that you saw wake in your writing
with meaning given to sweet melodies
and, sweeter, those unheard.
Unravished bride in the pastoral cold!

You knew that this mask (a mold of your face
to hold back your life) was not Her,
was not the Form of Poetry you waited for,
as if summer days would never cease.
You knew She would come in sudden power
to find you a serene Dionysus,
a wrenched and turbulent Apollo.
And when She came, She would wreathe the band of flowers
that binds us to earth, this melancholy earth,
which, in Autumn, gathering swallows soar above
and vanish twittering along a curved sky.

But different was the mask within.
Carnality, and blood, the sense of being,
thought knifing into things,
anguish, love, death that glides by so close,
and the thing of beauty, a joy forever,
all this throbbed inside,
never did oppress or kill you,
but found refuge in the gloom, distilling
warmth blown down to us from a distant star,
or murmuring within the serene well of memory.
All this was identical, particular, unmoved,
strange or shapeless,
unknown, unmoveable, or silent.

It was this mask you wore, the day they fit you.
It was not the mask of the man you were
and which bronze covered as if man
was only a mask for poet!
No artist could have seen the other mask,
only you. No mold could have captured this,
if you hadn't closed your eyes half in love
with easeful death, and sealed mouth and lips
calmly as eyelids finally at rest but
forever yearning — and forever silent,
the look that seemed about to speak.

Lisbon, 6 June 1959

Dancer from Brunei

to Ruy Cinatti

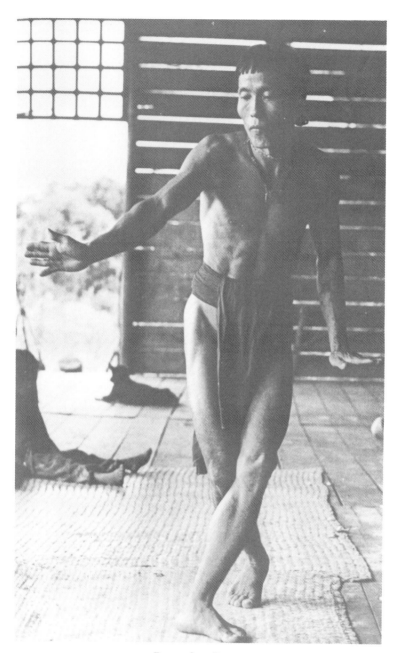

Dancer from Brunei
Photo by Dean Conger, Dir. of Photography, *National Geographic*
By kind permission of the National Geographic Society

In strong lines of smooth contours
and in steps arranged to stretch
the gesture of almost complete nudity
(no, complete, for nothing is hidden
or dressed up by the slight cloth
dangling from his waist), in the nudity
of this body rippling strong but fragile
as though languid from loving, dance
itself balances upon a moment
in this quiet image. Feet
settle down: one on tip-toe, the other
crossed before the thigh's gentle torque.
Cheekbones and focused eyes seem to flow
like the bangs of hair in this bronze
relief, side-lit. On his chest
rising from his waist, a necklace
marks the lines of the collar
where the head is held erect, delicate.
He figures forth a primitive tribe
in Borneo. An elegance from
centuries of human perfecting
that a people make in their knowing life.
When will it be that from the west death
comes to kill us before we kill
not just the god-become-men
but the men-become-gods
who already are so few, yet so limpid,
as this body dancing in itself
(the ready hands securing fast the air)?

19 January 1974

Death, Space, and Eternity

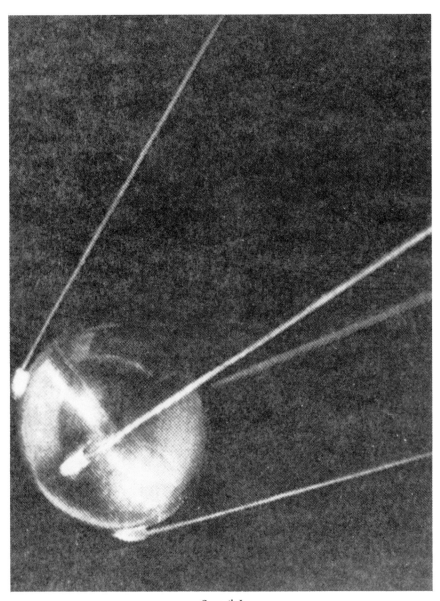

Sputnik I

No one ever died a natural death.
We were not born to die, not for death
do we catch the hollow murmur,
the irremediable, expiring howling
from the times we were amphibians moving
along a shore, or were standing quadrihuman.
No. It was not for our dying that we spoke,
discovered tenderness and fire,
painting, writing, sweet music.
It was not to die that we dreamed
of being immortal, having a soul, living again,
dreamed, for our own sake, of gods more
immortal that we could dream. No.
But when the unspeakable end of flesh
seems natural, within the order of things
or of angels; when it weighs us down
as an insatiable hunger for the infinite;
when it seems willed by the other gods
who are only faces of the one; and when pain
is a human error we give in to, out of pain,
and something of us is lost in others; then
we betray the upward journey, the victory,
the being, step by step, more human.

In nature, death is natural. But we
deny nature. We are the species denial,
the negation of everything binding us
to Sun, earth, water.
We were born to rise up. Against everything
and beyond whatever is always the same,

born and dying, born and dying, ending
as extinct specimens of other eras.
It was for our rising up free that death
gave us fear for destiny. Everything
is done to flee it, everything
imagined to fool it, everything —
courage, detachment, love —
just so death could be natural.

It is not. How could it be, if,
knowing it, suffering it, living it
for millions of years, we can still
refuse it, even when murdering? Why
has no one welcomed it, except
when worn out with living? Why
can no one conceive of it
for the beloved, a separate essence, a body
loved more than ourselves? How,
when the animals, much like us,
reveal it in a bitter languid,
rebelling gaze flickering away?

We have always died. Which proves?
Stars die, coming to an end. Everything
that ends, they say, dies. Which proves?
Only that we die of a tiny universe,
or a universe only conquered in tiny bits.

Life has no limits. Not the life
that leapt into being one day
when crystals began to eat;
nor the animal or vegetable life,
always a constant dying
of lives nourishing other lives
so that new life might arise
absorbing primitive cells.

But Human Life, the breathed,
sweated, discharged, circulated life
of shit and blood, seed
and pleasure and pain and skin that throbs
easy and cool beneath ardent fingers.
This has no limits.
It is unjust we still die, no longer
dying from so much that used to kill.
It is the tiny bit of universe
that those who possess everything cling to,
so that they will be able to die.
That tiny bit is not enough, it kills us
when Life, copying it, does not abound
but shrinks like the pelt of a wild ass:
malleable, submissive, resigned.
Death is an injustice. And anyone
who acquiesces to its coming is a coward.
Eternal complacency is the natural state,
a betrayal of the fear through which we are,
a betrayal of our condition, which is
to be, of the infinite Universe,
the spirit always more vast.

The Sun, the Milky Way, the Nebulae,
we will have them all, see them all,
until the moment when Life is for
the immortals we are when freed from death.
Death is for this world where sin,
fall, original faultiness, and evil
are the subdued acceptance of what will be.

And God wants none of us, not one of us,
to be accepting. He waits,
like a judge at the finish line,
wringing hands in despair and anguish
because he can do nothing, seeing

the runner give up, ease into comfort,
or fall exhausted along the way.
From us, God increases and becomes
the spirit that we are, and the knowledge
and the strength. We will not rest in his arms;
he will be found in ours
reaching farther than he ever has.
God does not watch over us — me, you, those
you love, those loved by you, those who made you —
no, there is no watching over us. By each death
we yield to, God feels robbed,
gnawed by the rats of that demon:
the natural man who accepts death
and nature made of death.

When the time comes, when everything on earth
has already been human — flesh and blood —
there will be no one to blow the trumpet
calling the globe to a single formless body,
a single desire, a single love, a single sex.
The earth being us, and we being the earth
and closed upon it, resurrection is death
for that God waiting for us
to fill out his Universal spirit and flesh.
We were born to rise. We see, outlined
by our dread, this clear destiny:
worlds may end, but Life,
lifted into other spaces, other worlds,
will find places to continue.
And when the infinite should no longer
exist, and should we find its limit,
Life with its fists will thrust it forward
so Eternity will fit in Space.

Assis, 1 April 1961, Holy Saturday

Post-Metamorphosis

First Variation

In burning sun, in blue sea, in wind
that thrills their skin, the gods mingle
in the complete nakedness of wild youth,
displaying impudent passion
for any spying human eyes.

They are promiscuous, falling in a rush
of bodies, legs, arms, mouths and hair,
hips and hands, tongues and moans,
spasmodic ecstasies, breasts and shudders,
and sex is all that is delivered and all
that in sure rhythm elicits jerks
(the deep adjusting to the rigid)
and leaks away and begins again.
Bodies are wrung, pitch and heave,
rise a bit and arch and fall,
and slowly become placid
as if sleeping in the spreading, anonymous
divine confusion of a finish.

Suddenly, the most high get up,
near bodies still lying, quivering.
Others get up, too, outlined by light
that makes the black of their sex iridescent.
The bright beach echoes with guffaws
and with serene cascades of surf
licking the sand left behind
as if poised on the threshold of wind.

The gods run to the sea — a brief splash.
Yet one lingers where sand and water meet,
lounging, stretching out arms over
curving hips and taut legs sprinkled
with foam ankles are drenched in.
He gives a shout, rushes and plunges in the wake
of the others, now points in the distance
or only shadows of tiny waves breaking,
far away, against the light.

Gliding elegant sylphs ironically
smooth away any physical traces from the beach
— disturbed sand, vague prints
of haunch and chest, heels and napes,
scattered drops of spilled love.

Promiscuous is the love of gods (whenever
spied on by human eyes, thirsty and bothered)
and dissolute, violent, abrupt.
Only echoes of laughter
remain and, in our memory, the shape
of a god lounging where sand and water meet.

Lisbon, 2 May 1959

Second Variation

Caryatid, taut, that your body is
in anxious expectation of remembered pleasure,
you support, on immeasureable shoulders
and unfolded hands, the husky inspiring flight
that envelops smooth fine skin
and flesh, rosy and dense, in which
focused hard blood attentively pulses.
Poised on feet — and upon your shoulders every
invisible thing woven by the quivering
of your fingers — you support haunches, legs,
breasts, bush, a lost glance, and arms and hair.

Caryatid, your desires undulate you!
Thus standing on your parted legs,
on the wing-like curve that, from chin to belly,
lengthens the world that moves upon your fingers
like round placid buttocks of azure sky,
to rest upon the horizon
of nubile hips, you support
the whirl of planets. And geometry,
in axes of torso and sex, inscribes
the gesture with which pendulant hips
revolve around themselves, held
between columns that make a column
of the moistened statue that you are.
Void gaze, O demolished temple,
O shattered roof, O hacked-apart dark,
O variable and perfect form
of what there is and is not! O caryatid!
Pillar of the world! How tender the arm

falling from your shoulder! How frail
the firm decision that rests upon you,
from shoulders to waist, from waist to legs,
from spread legs to flattened foot
that sits delicately upon time
slipping away in leaps of desire
that contract you, lick you, and slide off
onto the ground of things and the dust
a breeze raises in clouds
around your face. When . . .
When ending, when blood returns to you,
when ejaculating brilliance
of stars crowning your hair,
when, caryatid, your breasts are
the source from which that universe
drips down, which finitely gnaws
the absent fringe of unlimited nothing,
you sustain, full but already diminutive,
in the curve of your lips, in the saliva
that between them petrifies taut tongues,
you sustain everything in your white teeth:
the returning of time, the repelling
of the husky inspiring and strange gesture
completely running through you,
mistress of destiny, congealed life,
whom a touch liquefies, salty and fine,
in blood dense and black, in unfolded hands,
in linear fingers stroking space.

Araraquara, 7 March 1962